SHAKESPEARE FOR YOUNG PEOPLE

HAMLET

HENRY THE FIFTH

JULIUS CAESAR

MACBETH

A MIDSUMMER NIGHT'S DREAM

MUCH ADO ABOUT NOTHING

ROMEO AND JULIET

THE TAMING OF THE SHREW

THE TEMPEST

TWELFTH NIGHT

SHAKESPEARE ON STAGE

AS YOU LIKE IT

HAMLET

JULIUS CAESAR

MACBETH

THE MERCHANT OF VENICE

A MIDSUMMER NIGHT'S DREAM

OTHELLO, THE MOOR OF VENICE

ROMEO AND JULIET

Viola: (Speaking of her own love for him.) My
father had a daughter loved a man . . . as it
might be, perhaps, were I a woman,
I should your lordship.

SHAKESPEARE FOR YOUNG PEOPLE

TWELFTH NIGHT

by
William Shakespeare

edited and illustrated by
Diane Davidson

SWAN BOOKS
A division of Learning Links Inc
New Hyde Park, New York

Published by
SWAN BOOKS
a division of
LEARNING LINKS INC.
2300 Marcus Avenue
New Hyde Park, NY 11042

Printed in the United States of America

Library of Congress Cataloging-in-Publication Data

Shakespeare, William, 1564–1616
Twelfth Night
(Shakespeare for young people)
Summary: An abridged version of Shakespeare's original text,
with suggestions for staging. Includes parenthetical explanations
and descriptions within the text and announcers who summarize deleted
passages.
1. Children's plays, English. [1. Plays] I. Davidson, Diane.
II. Title.   III. Series: Shakespeare, William, 1564–1616.
Shakespeare for young people
PR2837. A25 1996 822.3′3—dc20   96—19754
ISBN 978-07675-0874-2

TO THE TEACHER OR PARENT

Young people can grow up loving Shakespeare if they act out his plays. Since Shakespeare wrote for the theater, not for the printed page, he is most exciting on his own ground.

Many people are afraid that the young will not understand Shakespeare's words. To help these actors follow the story, the editor has added two optional announcers who introduce and explain scenes. However, young people pick up the general meaning with surprising ease, and they enjoy the words without completely understanding them at first. Their ears tell them the phrases often sound like music, and the plays are full of marvelous scenes.

After all, Shakespeare is not called the best of all writers because he is hard. He is the best of all writers because he is enjoyable.

HOW TO BEGIN

At first, students may find the script too difficult to enjoy, so one way to start is for the director to read the play aloud. Between scenes, ask, "What do you think is going to happen next?" or "Do you think the characters should do this?" After the students become familiar with the story and words, they can try out for parts by reading different scenes. In the end, the director should pick those who are the best actors, emphasizing, "There are no small parts. Everybody helps in a production."

The plays can be presented in several ways.

In the simplest form, the students can read the script aloud, sitting in their seats. This will do well enough, but it is more fun to put on the actual show.

What can a director do to help the actors?

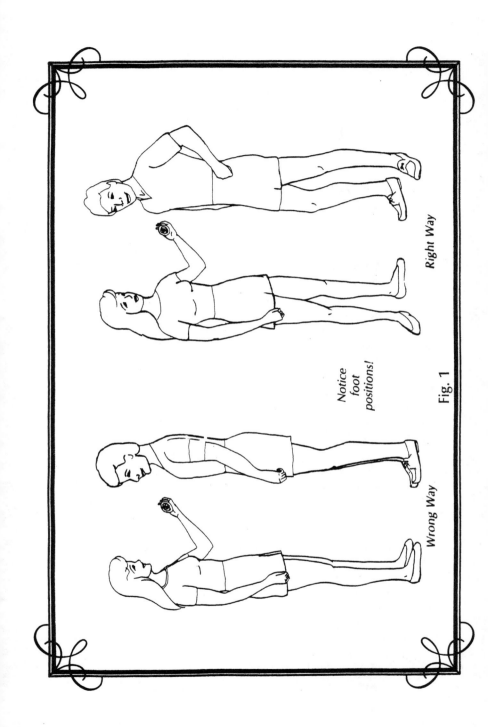

Wrong Way

Notice foot positions!

Right Way

Fig. 1

One main point is to have the actors speak more slowly than usual. They should not be afraid to pause or to emphasize short phrases. However, they should not try to be "arty" or stilted. Shakespeare wrote very energetic plays.

A second main point in directing is to keep the students facing the audience, even if they are talking to someone else. They should "fake front," so that their bodies face the audience and their heads are only half-way towards the other actors. (Fig. 1)

The cast should be told that when the announcers speak between scenes, servants can continue to change the stage set, and actors can enter, exit, or stand around pretending to talk silently. But if an announcer speaks during a scene, the actors should "freeze" until the announcer has finished the lines. At no time should the actors look at the announcers. (The announcers' parts may be cut out if the director so desires.)

Encouragement and applause inspire the young to do better, and criticism should always be linked with a compliment. Often letting the students find their own way through the play produces the best results. And telling them, "Mean what you say," or "Be more energetic!" is all they really need.

SCHEDULES AND BUDGETS

Forty-five minutes a day—using half the time for group scenes and half the time for individual scenes—is generally enough for students to rehearse. The director should encourage all to learn their lines as soon as possible. An easy way to memorize lines is to tape them and have the student listen to the tape at home each evening, going over it four or five times. Usually actors learn faster by ear than by eye. In all, it takes about six weeks to prepare a good show.

The play seems more complete if it has an audience, even other people from next door. But an afternoon or evening public performance is better yet. The director should announce the show well in advance. A PTA meeting, Open House, a Renaissance Fair, a holiday—all are excellent times to do a play.

To attract a good crowd, the admission should be very small or free. However, a Drama Fund is always useful, so some groups pass a hat, or parents sell cookies and punch. But the best way to raise money for a Drama Fund is to sell advertising in the program. A business-card size ad can sell for $5 to $10, and a larger ad brings in even more. This is money gained well in advance of the show. It can be used for costumes or small 250-500 watt spotlights that can be mounted anywhere. Until there is money in the Drama Fund, the director often becomes an expert at borrowing and improvising. Fortunately, Shakespeare's plays can be produced with almost no scenery or special costumes, and there are no royalties to pay.

SPECIAL NOTES ON THIS PLAY

Twelfth Night needs only simple staging: two 'wings' or screens on each side of the playing area and a couple of screens making an open alcove at the back. If possible, use the school stage. But good shows can take place at one end of a room. (Fig. 2)

What can people use as screens? Tall cardboard refrigerator boxes are good. Stage flats, frames of 1″ x 4″ lumber joined by triangles of plywood and covered with muslin sheeting, are excellent if little side flats are hinged to the main one, to provide bracing.

The alcove along the back indicates scenes by lengths of painted cardboard or simple props. (Fig 3) Benches on either side of the alcove complete the scenery. On each side of the stage should be chairs for the announcers.

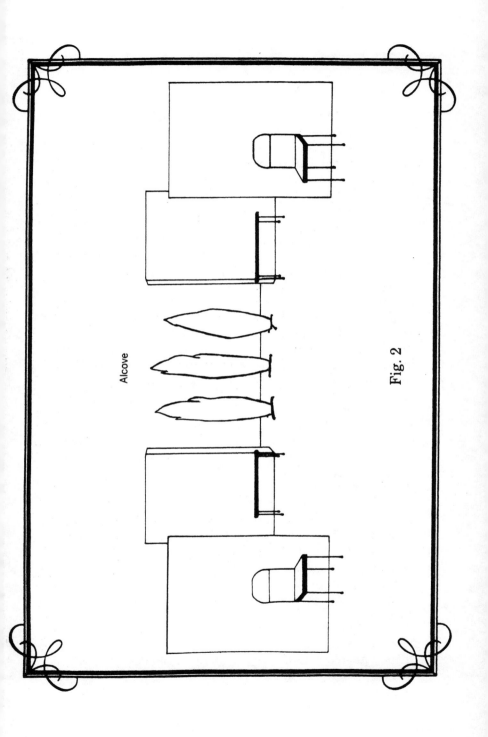

Alcove

Fig. 2

The director should decide where actors enter and exit, having one side of the stage generally represent the direction of the Duke's palace and the other side Olivia's house.

Twelfth Night is usually performed in medieval or Renaissance costumes. Draperies make excellent material, often donated by thrift shops or dry cleaners with unclaimed goods. The Duke and Sir Toby can wear long or short robes as desired. Malvolio wears a very severe black suit with a big Puritan collar. Other men wear short pants with tights, plus full blouses (ladies' blouses, belted, with sleeves puffed by elastic bands, do very well), or page-boy outfits. Ladies' dresses have full-length skirts, and Olivia should be dressed in black for mourning. Viola and her twin Sebastian should be dressed identically, with some little difference (she could have a red feather in her hat, and he could have a blue one). Her suit should also have a detachable skirt that she wears at the beginning.

A word of warning is necessary: the duel is fought with cardboard swords, but no one should play with them.

In acting, to "blow a kiss," first kiss the fingertips, then extend the hand a little, palm upward, and puff a breath across the fingertips toward the beloved.

For background music, something happy like a Mozart symphony is excellent. The first movement is always quick, and the second movement is slower and romantic.

A LAST BIT OF ADVICE

How will a director know if he or she has produced Shakespeare "correctly"? Ask the group if they had fun. If they answer, "Yes," then the show is a success.

ALCOVE SCENERY

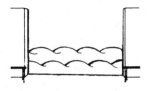

Stormy Sea

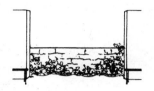

City Wall with Flowers
(Reverse of Stormy Sea)

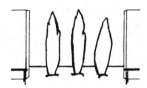

Lady Olivia's Garden
(Cardboard cypress trees in
Christmas tree stands)

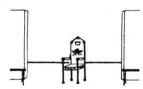

The Duke's Palace

Malvolio's Prison Bars

Fig. 3

CHARACTERS

Two Announcers (optional), who have been added

The Duke's Household
Orsino [Or-**see**-no], the lovesick Duke of Illyria
[Ill-**leer**-ee-uh]
Valentine ⎫ gentlemen
Curio [**Cure**-ee-oh ⎭ of the Duke's court

Olivia's Household
Olivia, a beautiful young countess in mourning
Maria, Olivia's maid
Sir Toby Belch, Olivia's fat drunken uncle
Sir Andrew Aguecheek (**Ay**-gyu-cheek], Sir Toby's
silly friend, in love with Olivia
Malvolio [Mal-**voh**-lee-oh], Olivia's fussy, Puritanical
steward or house-manager
Fabian [**Fay**-bee-un], a servant of Olivia's
Feste [Fest], a clown and singer, Olivia's jester

Strangers in Illyria
Viola, a ship-wrecked beautiful young lady
Sea Captain, friend to Viola
Sebastian, Viola's handsome twin brother
Antonio, a sea captain and friend of Sebastian's

People of Illyria
Two Officers, the local police
Priest
Servants

ACT I

(In the alcove, the scenery shows a stormy sea. Two announcers enter, bow and take their places on each side of the stage area.)

Announcer 1: (To the audience) Welcome, everyone, to a production of Shakespeare's *Twelfth Night* given by the _____ class. It is a comedy for the holidays.

Announcer 2: In olden times, on the twelfth night of Christmas, people played tricks on each other, as in this story.

Announcer 1: This is not the complete play but a shortened version, using the original words.

Announcer 2: The story begins in the romantic, far-off country of Illyria, where there has been a shipwreck. Viola and her twin brother, Sebastian, are separated by the storm.

(Thunder. Behind the cardboard waves, Viola and Sebastian are seen swimming. They wave farewell and sink. The Sea Captain swims on to lift Viola up and take her off. Sebastian surfaces with a cardboard log, swimming away in the other direction. Servants turn over the wave scenery to show a city wall with flowers.)

Announcer 1: Meanwhile in nearby Illyria, the storm is over, but a different storm begins. The young Duke is very much in love with a beautiful lady, Olivia.

The Duke enters, smelling a long-stemmed rose romantically. Valentine and Curio, his gentlemen, play music behind him. The Duke sighs. Olivia enters on the opposite side, crying into her handkerchief.)

Announcer 2: But Olivia's brother has just died. She is so sad that she swears not to get married for seven long years.

(The Duke tries to give Olivia a rose. She shakes her head and exits crying. The Duke gives the rose to Valentine and gestures for him to take it to Olivia. Valentine bows and exits.)

Duke: (To Curio) If music be the food of love, play on *(Curio plays. The Duke sighs.)* That strain again. It had a dying fall; *(Curio repeats the notes.)* O, it came o'er my ear like the sweet sound that breathes upon a bank of violets, stealing and giving odor. *(Curio stops as Valentine enters with the rose bent in half. The Duke looks at him.)* How now? What news from her?

Valentine: So please my lord, I do return this answer. *(He gives him the broken rose.)* Till seven years hence, she will season a brother's dead love!

Announcer 1: The Duke thinks that so much love for a brother means Olivia will love a husband even more. Especially himself.

Duke: (Very impressed) O, she hath a heart of that fine frame to pay this debt of love but to a brother. *(He looks after her.)* How will she love with . . . one self king. *(He blows a kiss to her and leaves hopefully with the others.)*

(Onto the stage come Viola and the Sea Captain.)

Viola: (Looking about) What country, friend, is this?

Captain: This is Illyria, lady.

Viola: (Sadly) And what should I do in Illyria? My brother, he is in Elysium. *(She shakes her head.)* Perchance he is not drowned. O my poor brother.

Captain: To comfort you, I saw your brother bind himself to a strong mast, where, like Arion on the dolphin's back, I saw him hold acquaintance with the waves so long as I could see.

Viola: (Happily giving him a coin) For saying so, there's gold. *(She looks about.)* Knowest thou this country? *(The Captain nods.)* Who governs here?

Captain: A noble duke, Orsino.

Viola: Orsino! I have heard my father name him. He was a bachelor then.

Captain: And was so very late. A month ago he did seek the love of fair Olivia, the daughter of a count that died, leaving her in the protection of her brother, who shortly also died. For whose dear love, they say, she hath abjured the sight and company of men.

Viola: O, that I served that lady.

Captain: (Shaking his head) She will admit no kind of suit, no, not the Duke's.

Announcer 2: But Viola needs a place to stay.

Announcer 1: She decides to disguise herself as a page boy and have the Captain recommend her to the Duke.

Viola: Captain, I prithee, conceal me what I am, and be my aid for such disguise. I'll serve this duke. Thou shalt present me to him, for I can sing and speak to him in many sorts of music that will allow me very worth his service. *(She tries to look brave.)*

Captain: (Putting his finger to his lips) Your mute I'll be.

Viola: I thank thee. Lead me on. *(He smiles with admiration as they leave to go to the Duke.)*

(Servants remove the city wall and put three cardboard cypress trees in the alcove.)

Announcer 2: In the Lady Olivia's garden, her drunken uncle, Sir Toby Belch, enjoys life.

(Sir Toby enters, sits on a bench with his beer mug, drinks deeply, and belches with satisfaction. Maria enters and frowns, her hands on her hips.)

Sir Toby: What a plague means to my niece, to take the death of her brother thus?

Maria: By my troth, Sir Toby, you must come in earlier o'nights. *(She walks to him, taking away his beer mug.)* Your cousin, my lady, takes great exception to your ill hours. And of a foolish knight that you brought in one night here to be her wooer.

Sir Toby: Who, Sir Andrew Aguecheek? Why, he has three thousand ducats a year.

Maria: (Saucily) He's a very fool. He's drunk nightly in your company.

Sir Toby: With drinking healths to my niece. *(He grabs back his beer mug.)* I'll drink to her as long as there is a passage in my throat and drink in Illyria. *(He puts his arm around Maria, but she pushes him away with a laugh.)* What, wench? *(He looks offstage.)* Here comes Sir Andrew Agueface.

Sir Andrew: (Entering) Sir Toby Belch. How now, Sir Toby Belch. *(Sir Toby rises and they slap each other on the back. Then Sir Andrew tries to kiss Maria.)* Bless you, fair shrew. *(She dodges him so he falls flat.)* Fair lady, do you think you have fools in hand?

Maria: Sir, I have not you by th' hand. Fare you well, gentlemen. *(With a toss of her head, she leaves, laughing. Sir Andrew looks forlorn.)*

Sir Toby: O knight, when did I see thee so put down?

Announcer 1: Sir Andrew has no luck trying to get Olivia to marry him.

Sir Andrew: (Rising) I'll ride home tomorrow, Sir Toby. Faith, your niece will not be seen. Or if she be, it's four to one she'll none of me.

Sir Toby: (He gives Sir Andrew the beer mug to encourage him.) Tut, there's life in it, man.

Sir Andrew: (After a deep drink.) I'll stay a month longer. *(Smiling)* I am a fellow of the strangest mind in the world. *(He takes another drink and does a dance step.)* I delight in masks and revels sometimes altogether.

Sir Toby: (Cheerfully) What is they excellence?

Sir Andrew: (Jumping and clicking his heels together) Faith, I can cut a caper. *(He dances around, doing fancy steps.)*

Sir Toby: Wherefore are those things hid? *(He takes his beer mug back as he tries to dance too.)* Let me see thee caper! *(Sir Andrew jumps about.)* Ha, higher, ha, ha, excellent! *(They dance offstage, roaring with laughter.)*

(The servants remove the trees and put on the throne.)

Announcer 2: In the Duke's palace, Viola is now known as the page boy Cesario. *(The Duke enters from one side and Viola, dressed as a page, from the other.)*

Duke: (Looking about) Who saw Cesario, ho?

Viola: (Bowing) On your attendance, my lord.

Duke: (In confidence) Cesario, thou knowest all. I have unclasped to thee my secret soul. *(Viola nods.)*

Announcer 1: According to the customs of the time, the Duke wants the page Cesario to go to Olivia and plead for her to marry the Duke.

Duke: Therefore, good youth, stand at her doors.

Viola: (Doubtfully) Sure, my noble lord, she will never admit me.

Duke: (Urging Viola to make noise) Be clamourous. Unfold the passion of my love. Act my woes. *(He gives her a purse of money.)* Dear lad, prosper well in this.

Viola: (Bowing) I'll do my best to woo your lady. *(As she leaves, she gazes back at the Duke and puts her hand over her heart.)* Yet, a barful strife! Whoe'er I woo, myself would be his wife. *(She blows him a kiss. He does not notice as he too exits.)*

Announcer 2: So Viola, in love with the Duke herself, must try to get Olivia to marry him.

(The servants take off the throne and put on the trees. As they work, Maria and the Clown enter. The Clown frisks around, as Maria scolds lightly.)

Announcer 1: There is servant trouble at Olivia's house.

Maria: Nay, tell me where thou hast been. My lady will hang thee for thy absence.

Clown: (Mocking) Many a good hanging prevents a bad marriage.

Maria: Peace, you rogue. Here comes my lady. *(She leaves as Olivia enters with Malvolio, the sour-faced steward.)*

Clown: (Bowing) God bless thee, lady.

Olivia: (Displeased) Take the fool away.

Clown: (To an imaginary crowd) Do not hear, fellows? Take away the lady!

Olivia: Sir, I bade them take away you.

Clown: Good madonna, give me leave to prove you a fool.

Olivia: (Amused in spite of herself) Can you do it?

Clown: Good madonna, why mourn'st thou?

Olivia: (Sadly) Good fool, for my brother's death.

Clown: I think his soul is in Hell, madonna.

Olivia: I know his soul is in Heaven, fool.

Clown: The more fool, madonna, to mourn for your brother's soul being in Heaven. *(With a wide gesture)* Take away the fool, gentlemen.

Malvolio: (With scorn) I marvel your ladyship takes delight in such a rascal.

Olivia: (Displeased at his lack of humor) O, you are sick of self-love, Malvolio. *(She pats the fool on the head fondly.)* There is no slander in an allowed fool. *(The Clown grins.)*

Maria: (Entering in a rush Madam, there is at the gate a young gentleman much desires to speak with you.

Olivia: Go you, Malvolio. If it be a suit from the Count, I am sick or not at home. *(Malvolio exits as Sir Toby staggers in.)* By mine honor, half drunk.

Sir Toby: (Greeting the Clown) How now, sot!

Olivia: (With anger) Cousin, cousin.

Sir Toby: (With a shrug) Well, it's all one. *(He staggers off.)*

Olivia: (To the Clown, pointing after Sir Toby) Go seek my coz. He's drowned.

Clown: He is but mad, madonna, and the fool shall look to the madman. *(He skips off.)*

Malvolio: (Entering with a frown) Madam, yon young fellow swears he will speak with you. I told him you were sick. He takes on him to understand so much, and therefore comes to speak with you. I told him you were asleep. He seems to have a foreknowledge of that too, and therefore comes to speak with you. What is to be said to him, lady?

Olivia: Of what personage and years is he?

Malvolio: Not yet old enough for a man nor young enough for a boy.

Olivia: Let him approach. *(Malvolio leaves as Maria enters.)* Give me my veil. *(Olivia sits on a bench, and Maria puts the veil over her face.)*

Viola: (Entering and looking around) The honorable lady of the house, which is she?

Olivia: Speak to me, I shall answer for her.

Viola: (Taking out a little paper, checking it, and starting to read it.) Most radiant, exquisite, and unmatchable beauty . . . *(She stops and asks Maria for help, pointing to Olivia.)* I pray you, tell me if this be the lady of the house, for I never saw her.

Olivia: Whence came you, sir?

Viola: (Looking at her notes) I can say little more than I have studied, and that question's out of my part.

Olivia: Are you a comedian?

Viola: No. Are you the lady of the house?

Olivia: (Amused) I am.

Viola: (Bowing) I will on with my speech in your praise. *(She hesitates.)* It alone concerns your ear. *(She points to Maria, who is listening.)*

Olivia: (To Maria) Give us this place alone. *(Maria exits.)* Now, sir where lies your text?

Viola: (Romantically) In Orsino's heart.

Olivia: (Bored) O, I have read it. Have you no more to say? *(She yawns.)*

Viola: (Pertly) Good madam, let me see your face.

Olivia: You are now out of your text. But we will draw the curtain and show you the picture. *(She throws back her veil.)* Look you, sir. Is't not well done?

Viola: (Inspecting her face closely for makeup.) Excellently done, if God did all.

Olivia: (Rubbing her face with her handkerchief and showing Viola the result.) 'Twill endure wind and weather.

Viola: 'Tis beauty truly blent, whose red and white Nature's own sweet and cunning hand laid on.

Announcer 2: Viola thinks Olivia should marry and have children to inherit her beauty.

Viola: Lady, you are the cruellest she alive if you will lead these graces to the grave and leave the world no copy.

Olivia: Oh, sir, I will not be so hard-hearted. I will give out schedules of my beauty. It shall be inventoried—as, item, two lips, indifferent red. Item, two gray eyes, with lids to them. Item, one neck, one chin and so forth.

Viola: (Scolding) I see you what you are. You are too proud. But, if you were the devil, you are fair. My lord and master loves you.

Olivia: (Turning away coldly) Your lord does know my mind. I cannot love him.

Viola: (Kneeling beside her emotionally) If I did love you in my master's flame, with such a suffering, such a deadly life—in your denial I would find no sense. I would not understand it!

Olivia: (Affected by Viola's appeal) Why what would you?

Announcer 1: Viola tells how she would woo a lover.

Viola: *(Sitting on the ground, her back to the bench, she romantically gazes at the sky.)* Make me a willow cabin at your gate, and call upon my soul within the house. Write loyal cantons of condemned love and sing them loud even in the dead of night. Holla your name to the reverberate hills, and make the babbling gossip of the air cry out, "Olivia!" *(She signs with emotion.)* O, you should not rest between the elements of air and earth, but you should pity me.

(Olivia, much affected, starts to touch Viola's head. But she draws her hand back quickly to place it over her heart. She is falling in love with the page!)

Olivia: You might do much. *(Trying to be calm)* What is your parentage?

Viola: *(Rising)* Above my fortunes, yet my state is well. I am a gentleman.

Olivia: *(Also rising)* Get you to your lord. *(She stammers a little.)* Let him send no more, unless you come to me again to tell me how he takes it. Fare you well.

Viola: Farewell, fair cruelty. *(She bows and exits. Olivia blows her a kiss as she goes, but Viola does not see it.)*

Olivia: *(Remembering)* "What is your parentage?" "Above my fortunes, yet my state is well. I am a gentleman." I'll be sworn thou art. *(She clasps her hands to her heart.)* Not too fast, soft, soft. *(Calling)* What ho, Malvolio! *(Quickly she takes a ring from her finger.)*

Malvolio: (Entering) Here, madam.

Olivia: (Pretending anger) Run after that same peevish messenger. He left this ring behind him. Tell him I'll none of it. *(She hands him the ring and pauses with a new idea.)* If that the youth will come this way tomorrow, I'll give him reasons for it. *(Urging him to hurry.)* Hie thee, Malvolio.

Malvolio: Madam, I will. *(He exits after Viola.)*

Olivia: (Confused, she shakes her head.) I do I know not what. *(She pulls off her mourning veil as she leaves, dancing a little and smiling.)*

ACT II

(The servants remove the trees and put the city wall in place. Antonio and Sebastian enter.)

Announcer 1: Viola's twin brother, Sebastian, comes to Illyria with a sea captain, Antonio, who rescued him.

Antonio: Will you stay no longer?

Sebastian: No, sir. You must know, Antonio, my name is Sebastian. My father left behind him myself and a sister, both born in an hour. Before you took me from the sea was my sister drowned.

Antonio: Alas the day!

Sebastian: A lady, sir, though it was said she much resembled me, was yet accounted beautiful. *(He sighs.)*

Antonio: (Good-heartedly) Let me be your servant.

Sebastian: (Shaking his head) I am bound to the Count Orsino's court. Farewell. *(They clasp hands and go separate ways.)*

(Viola enters with Malvolio following.)

Malvolio: (Calling) Were not you even now with the Countess Olivia?

Viola: (Turning to him) Even now, sir.

Malvolio: (Holding out the ring.) She returns this ring to you, sir. She adds, moreover, that you never come again, unless it be to report your lord's taking of this.

Viola: She took no ring of me. I'll none of it.

Malvolio: Come, sir, you peevishly threw it to her. And her will is, it should be so returned. *(He throws it at Viola.)* There it lies. *(He exits).*

Viola: (Picking up the ring from the ground) I left no ring with her. What means this lady? *(She looks at her page's suit.)* Fortune forbid my outside have not charmed her. *(With a gasp of surprise)* She loves me sure. Poor lady, she were better love a dream.

(Shaking her head at the puzzle) My master loves her dearly, and I, poor monster, fond as much on him. And she, mistaken, seems to dote on me. What will become of this? *(Looking up at the sky helplessly)* O Time, thou must untangle this, not I. It is too hard a knot for me to untie. *(She leaves, confused.)*

(The servants remove the city wall and put up the cypress trees. Sir Toby and Sir Andrew come in, beer mugs in hand, yawning and drunken.)

Announcer 2: Poor Viola is in the middle of a love triangle. And to add to the problems, Sir Toby is having a noisy drunken party.

Sir Toby: Sir Andrew, not to be abed after midnight is to be up betimes. *(He hiccups.)*

Sir Andrew: I know, to be up late is to be up late. *(He drinks).*

O MISTRESS MINE

music by Diane Davidson

Sir Toby: Let us therefore eat and drink. *(Calling loudly for Maria)* Marian, I say! A stoup of wine!

Clown: (Entering) How now, my hearts?

Sir Toby: Come, let's have a song! A love song.

Clown: (Sings)

> O mistress mine, where are you roaming?
> O, stay and hear. Your true-love's coming,
>   That can sing both high and low.
> Trip no further, pretty sweeting;
> Journeys end in lovers' meeting,
>   Every wise man's son doth know.
>
> What is love? 'Tis not hereafter.
> Present mirth hath present laughter;
>   What's to come is still unsure;
> In delay there lies no plenty;
> Then, come kiss me, sweet-and-twenty,
>   Youth's a stuff will not endure.

Sir Toby: (Applauding) It is dulcet. *(He sings badly.)* "O, the twelfth day of December. . . ."

(Sir Andrew joins him with joy. They dance and act out the Christmas gifts in the old song. The Clown sings too, as they "pipe" and "drum," etc. Maria enters sleepily, followed by Malvolio in his night robe.)

Maria: (Shouting) For the love of God, peace!

Malvolio: My masters, are you mad? Do you make an ale-house of my lady's house?

Sir Toby: (Pulling Malvolio's nose) Sneck-up.

Malvolio: (Very sternly) Sir Toby, my lady bade me tell you that she is very willing to bid you farewell. *(He points to the exit.)*

Maria: (Trying to quiet him) Nay, good Sir Toby. *(She takes away his beer mug and puts it on a bench.)*

Sir Toby: (Imitating Malvolio's prissy voice.) Dost though think, because thou art "virtuous," there shall be no more cakes and ale? *(He dances a jig with the Clown, whooping.)* A stoup of wine, Maria!

Malvolio: (Scolding Maria) Mistress Mary, if you prized my lady's favor, you would not give means for this uncivil rule. She shall know of this. *(He shakes his fist in her face and leaves.)*

Maria: (Shouting after Malvolio) Go shake your ears. *(To Sir Toby)* Sweet Sir Toby, be patient for tonight. *(She feels insulted.)* For Monsieur Malvolio, sometimes he is a kind of Puritan. He thinks that all that look on him love him. *(Getting an idea)* And on that vice in him will my revenge work.

Announcer 1: Maria plans to play a Twelfth Night trick on Malvolio.

Announcer 2: She will drop a love letter where he will find it.

Sir Toby: (Grinning) What wilt thou do?

Maria: (Grinning back) I will drop in his way some epistles of love. I can write very like my lady, your niece . . .

Sir Toby: Excellent. He shall think by the letters that thou wilt drop that they come from my niece, and that she's in love with him!

Sir Andrew: O, 'twill be admirable.

Maria: Sport royal. I will plant you two, and let the fool make a third, where he shall find the letter. *(They all laugh and shake hands.)* For this night, to bed. Farewell. *(She leaves. The men look after her in admiration.)*

Sir Andrew: She's a good wench.

Sir Toby: She's a beagle, true-bred, and one that adores me. *(He blows a kiss after her and then nudges Sir Andrew.)* Send for more money. *(He yawns.)* Come, come, 'tis too late to go to bed now. Come, knight, come. *(They lurch offstage together happily.)*

(The servants take away the trees and the mug and put on the throne. The Duke, Viola, and Curio enter.)

Announcer 1: In the palace, Viola is still having problems being in love with the Duke, who loves Olivia, who loves Viola.

Announcer 2: The Duke calms his feelings with sad music about lost love.

Duke: Give me some music. That piece of song, that old and antique song we heard last night.

Curio: He is not here that should sing it. Feste, the jester, that the Lady Olivia's father took much delight in.

Come Away, Come Away, Death

Duke: Seek him out. *(Curio exits. The Duke puts his arm around Viola.)* Come hither, boy. If ever thou shalt love, in the sweet pangs of it remember me. *(Music plays.)* How dost thou like this tune?

Viola: (Sighing, her hand to her heart.) It gives a very echo to the seat where Love is throned.

Duke: (Thinking his page has been in love) Young though thou art, thine eye hath stayed upon some favour that it loves. Hath it not, boy?

Viola: (Shyly) A little.

Duke: What kind of woman is it?

Viola: Of your complexion.

Duke: She is not worth thee, then. What years, in faith?

Viola: About your years, my lord.

Duke: Too old, by Heaven. Let thy love be younger than thyself. *(He sees Olivia's clown Feste enter.)* O, fellow, come, the song we had last night. Prithee, sing.

Clown: (Sings)

Come away, come away, death,
　　And in sad cypress let me be laid.
Fly away, fly away, breath,
　　I am slain by a fair cruel maid.
My shroud of white, stuck all with yew,
　　O, prepare it!
My part of death, no one so true
　　Did share it.

Not a flower, not a flower sweet,
  On my black coffin let there be strown;
Not a friend, not a friend greet
  My poor corpse, where the bones shall be
    thrown.
A thousand thousand sighs to save,
  Lay me, O where
Sad true love never find my grave,
  To weep there.

(All applaud, while Viola weeps quietly. The Duke gives money to the Clown, who bows and leaves.)

Duke: (To his courtiers) Let all the rest give place. *(They bow and leave also.)*

Announcer 2: The Duke again sends Viola to woo Olivia for him.

Announcer 1: Viola almost tells him that she loves him herself.

Duke: Once more Cesario, get thee to yond same sovereign cruelty. Tell her my love.

Viola: But if she cannot love you, sir?

Duke: I cannot be so answered.

Viola: But you must. Say that some lady, as perhaps there is, hath for your love as great a pang of heart as you have for Olivia. You cannot love her. You tell her so. Must she not, then, be answered?

Announcer 1: The Duke does not believe women can love strongly.

Duke: There is no woman's heart so big, to hold so much. Mine is all as hungry as the sea.

Viola: Ay, but I know too well women are as true of heart as we. *(Speaking of her own love for him.)* My father had a daughter loved a man as it might be, perhaps, were I a woman, I should your lordship.

Announcer 2: Viola tells of the pale girl with the broken heart. She sat silent and still as a statue of Patience.

Duke: And what's her history?

Viola: A blank, my lord. She never told her love, but let concealment, like a worm i' the bud, feed on her damask cheek. She pined in thought. And, with a green and yellow melancholy, she sat like "Patience on a monument," smiling at grief. Was not this love indeed?

Duke: But died thy sister of her love, my boy?

Viola: (Mysteriously) I am all the daughters of my father's house, and all the brothers too. And yet I know not. *(Suddenly careful)* Sir, shall I to this lady?

Duke: Aye, to her in haste. *(He hands Viola a ring.)* Give her this jewel. *(Viola bows as the Duke leaves. She blows him another kiss and exits sadly.)*

(Servants take off the throne and put on the three trees of Olivia's garden. Sir Toby enters with Sir Andrew and Fabian, another courtier.)

Announcer 1: Sir Toby and his friends plan to trick Malvolio with the false love letter.

Sir Toby: Come thy ways, Signior Fabian. We will fool him black and blue.

Maria: (Entering in a hurry) Get ye all three into the box-tree. Malvolio's coming down this walk. *(She takes a folded note out of her pocket.)* I know this letter will make a contemplative idiot of him. *(Throwing the note on the ground.)* Lie thou there. *(She exits, giggling.)*

(The three men hide behind the cypress trees, poking their heads out halfway to watch Malvolio approach.)

Announcer 2: Malvolio enters, dreaming about being married to Lady Olivia.

Malvolio: 'Tis but fortune; all is fortune. To be Count Malvolio. *(He sighs at the thought.)*

Sir Toby: (In a whisper) Ah, rogue!

Malvolio: Having been three months married to her, sitting in my state—calling my officers about me, in my velvet gown, to ask for my kinsman Toby—

Sir Toby: (Hissing furiously) Bolts and shackles!

Malvolio: I frown the while, and perchance wind up my watch or play with some rich jewel. Toby approaches, curtsies there to me—

Sir Toby: (In a rage) Shall this fellow live?

Malvolio: I extend my hand to him thus, saying, "Cousin Toby, you must amend your drunkenness." *(He shakes his finger at him.)*

Sir Toby: Out, scab! *(He comes from behind his tree with his hands out to choke Malvolio. The other two pull him back behind the cypress as Malvolio sees the letter.)*

Malvolio: (Taking up the letter.) What employment have we here? *(After a close look)* By my life, this is my lady's hand. These be her very C's, her U's, and her T's. *(He opens the note and gasps with delight.)* "To the unknown beloved!" *(He kisses the letter with a loud smack and reads it.)*

> "Jove knows I love,
> But who?
> Lips, do not move;
> No man must know."

(Excited) If this should be thee, Malvolio?

Sir Toby: (Shaking his fist) Hang thee!

Malvolio: (Reading on)

> "I may command where I adore,
> But silence, like a Lucrece
> knife,
> With bloodless stroke my heart doth gore.
> M, O, A, I, doth sway my life."

Fabian: A riddle!

Malvolio: "M, O, A, I, doth sway my life." Nay, but first, let me see, let me see, let me see. *(He starts to think*

Malvolio: My lady loves me!

very hard.) "I may command where I adore." Why, she may command me. I serve her. She is my lady. *(He pats his hair and straightens his clothes.)* And the end—if I could make that resemble something in me! Softly, M, O, A, I. . . . "M."—Malvolio. "M" Why that begins my name.

Fabian: Did I not say he would work it out? *(The others nod gleefully. Then, carrying their trees, they creep halfway towards Malvolio to listen.)*

Malvolio: "M". . . . But then "A" should follow, but "O" does. *(He frowns.)* And then "I" comes behind. *(He scratches his head.)* M, O, A, I. . . . Every one of these letters are in my name.

(He turns the paper over and reads the back. The trees crowd around him.) Soft here follows prose. "In my stars I am above thee, but be not afraid of greatness. *(Slowly)* Some are born great, some achieve greatness, and some have greatness thrust upon 'em.

Announcer 2: The love letter tells Malvolio to be rude to Toby and to dress and act certain ways.

Malvolio: (Reading) "Be opposite with a kinsman. Remember who commended thy yellow stockings and wished to see thee ever cross-gartered. I say, remember." My lady loves me. *(Very excited, looking at his legs.)* She did not commend my yellow stockings of late. She did praise my leg being cross-gartered. *(He presses the letter to his heart.)* I am happy.

(Looking again at the letter) Here is yet a post-script. *(He reads.)* "Thou canst not choose but know who I am. Thy smiles become thee well. Therefore

in my presence still smile, dear my sweet." *(He stretches his face into a forced smile.)* I will smile. I will do everything that thou wilt have me! *(Smiling with all his teeth, he stalks offstage, waving the letter.)*

(The three men come out from behind the trees, laughing and capering as they put their trees back.)

Sir Toby: I could marry this wench for this device. *(Maria enters, and Sir Toby whirls her around.)* Why, thou hast put him in such a dream that he must run mad.

Maria: Nay, but say true. Does it work upon him? *(They cheer noisily.)* If you will then see the sport, mark his approach before my lady. He will come to her in yellow stockings, cross-gartered, a fashion she detests. *(She makes a face.)* And he will smile upon her, which will now be so unsuitable . . . *(She makes another face.)* that it cannot but turn him into a notable contempt. If you will see it, follow me.

Sir Toby: Thou most excellent devil. *(He kisses her cheek noisily, and they all follow Malvolio to see the fun.)*

ACT III

(On comes Olivia with Viola following. Sir Andrew re-turns and hides behind a tree, eavesdropping. Olivia and Viola sit.)

Olivia: Give me your hand, sir. *(Viola obeys shyly.)* What is your name?

Viola: Cesario, fair princess.

Olivia: You are servant to the Count Orsino, youth. *(Viola nods.)* I pray you, never speak again of him.

Viola: Then westward-ho! *(She starts to leave.)*

Olivia: (Rising and clutching Viola's arm.) Stay. *(Viola turns.)* Tell me what you think'st of me.

Viola: That you do think you are not what you are.

Olivia: If I think so, I think the same of you.

Viola: Then think you right. I am not what I am.

Olivia: (Desperately) Cesario, by the roses of the spring, by maidhood, honor, truth, and everything, I love thee so. Love sought is good, but given unsought is better.

Viola: (Jerking her arm free from Olivia) By innocence I swear, and by my youth, I have one heart, one bosom, and one truth, and that no woman has. And so adieu, good madam.

(She runs off. Sir Andrew comes from behind the tree, furious. Olivia runs past him, weeping. Sir Toby enters with Fabian.)

Sir Andrew: (Angrily to Sir Toby) No, faith, I'll not stay a jot longer. Marry, I saw your niece do favors to the Count's servingman. I saw it.

Sir Toby: Did she see thee the while?

Sir Andrew: As plain as I see you now.

Announcer 1: Fabian says Olivia wanted to make him jealous.

Fabian: (With a wink at Sir Toby) This was a great argument of love in her toward you. She did show favor to the youth in your sight to put fire in your heart. *(He punches the air.)* You should have banged the youth into dumbness.

Sir Toby: (Urging Sir Andrew on) Challenge the Count's youth to fight. Hurt him in eleven places.

Sir Andrew: Will either of you bear me a challenge to him? *(Both men nod vigorously.)*

Sir Toby: (Pushing him offstage) Go, write it in a martial hand. Be curst and brief. *(Sir Andrew draws his sword, waves it about, and leaves angrily.)*

Maria: (Pointing behind her) If you will laugh yourselves into stitches, follow me. Malvolio is in yellow stockings.

Sir Toby: (Grinning) And cross-gartered?

Maria: Most villainously. He does obey every point of the letter. He does smile his face into more lines than is in the new map with the augmentation of the Indies. I know my lady will strike him.

Sir Toby: Come, bring us, bring us where he is. *(They exit eagerly.)*

(Servants remove the trees and put up a city wall. Sebastian and Antonio enter.)

Announcer 2: Meanwhile Viola's twin brother Sebastian and his friend Antonio look around the town.

Announcer 1: But Antonio must not be seen, since he once fought in a war against the Duke.

Antonio: (Explaining) I could not stay behind you. These parts to a stranger often prove rough.

Sebastian: My kind Antonio, thanks. *(He looks about like a tourist.)* What's to do? I pray you, let us satisfy our eyes with the things of fame that do renown this city.

Antonio: (With an uneasy glance around) I do not without danger walk these streets. Once in a seafight 'gainst the Count, I did some service.

Sebastian: (Equally worried) Do not, then, walk too open.

Antonio: Hold sir, here's my purse. *(He gives him a bag of coins.)* In the south suburbs, at the Elephant, is best to lodge.

Sebastian: Why I your purse?

Antonio: Happily your eye shall light upon some toy you have desire to purchase.

Sebastian: (With a smile) I'll be your purse-bearer, and leave you for an hour.

Antonio: To the Elephant! *(They exit in different directions.)*

(The servants take off the city wall and put on the trees. Olivia enters, talking to herself. Behind her at a distance is Maria.)

Announcer 2: Olivia is so much in love that she sends for Viola again.

Olivia: (Upset) I have sent after him. He says he'll come. *(With a look at Maria)* I speak too loud. *(To Maria crossly)* Where is Malvolio?

Maria: (Pointing offstage) He's coming, madam, but in very strange manner. *(She twirls her finger at her temple.)* He does nothing but smile. Sure, the man is tainted in's wits.

(At first, all we see of Malvolio is one leg appearing, waving up and down. It has a yellow stocking and bright cross-garters. Then like a ballet dancer Malvolio leaps onto the stage after it and poses, showing off his criss-crossed yellow legs and smiling fantastically.)

Malvolio: (Loudly) Sweet lady, ho, ho!

Olivia: Smilest thou? I sent for thee upon a sad occasion.

Malvolio: (Quoting the letter) "Some are born great." *(He gives a little hop to one side.)* "Some achieve greatness." *(He gives a little hop to the other side.)* "And some have greatness thrust upon them!" *(He does a twirl and a bow.)*

Malvolio: Sad, lady? *(He looks painfully at his legs where the cross-garters are cutting off his circulation.)* I could be sad. This does make some obstruction in the blood, this cross-gartering. *(With a fresh smile)* but what of that? If it please the eye of one. *(He kisses his hand to her several times.)*

Olivia: What is the matter with thee? Why dost thou smile so, and kiss thy hand so oft?

Malvolio: (Quoting the letter) "Some are born great." *(He gives a little hop to one side.)* "Some achieve greatness." *(He gives a little hop to the other side.)* "And some have greatness thrust upon them!" *(He does a twirl and a bow.)*

Olivia: Heaven restore thee!

Malvolio: (With a wink, quoting more.) "Remember who commended thy yellow stockings."

Olivia: Thy yellow stockings?

Malvolio: "And wished to see them cross-gartered."

Olivia: Why, this is very midsummer madness.

Servant: (Entering) Madam, the young gentleman of the Count Orsino's is returned.

Olivia: I'll come to him. *(Pointing to Malvolio)* Good Maria, let this fellow be looked to. Where's Toby? *(She and Maria exit.)*

Malvolio: (In seventh heaven with happiness) O, ho. No worse man than Sir Toby to look to me. Nothing can come between me and my hopes.

Announcer 2: Sir Toby and the others decide to treat Malvolio like a madman and lock him up.

Sir Toby: (Entering with Maria and Fabian) Which way is he? *(Seeing Malvolio, he bursts into laughter.)*

Maria: Pray God he be not bewitched. Get him to say his prayers, good Sir Toby.

Malvolio: Go, hang yourselves all! You are idle shallow things. *(He flounces offstage.)*

Sir Toby: Come, we'll have him in a dark room, and bound. *(All nod.)* My niece is already in the belief that he's mad.

Announcer 1: Now Sir Toby and the others plan the duel between Sir Andrew and Viola.

Sir Andrew: (Entering and waving a paper) Here's the challenge; read it.

Sir Toby: (Reads) "Youth, I will waylay thee going home. Look to thyself, Andrew Aguecheek."

Maria: (Pointing offstage where Olivia went) He is now with my lady and will by and by depart.

Sir Toby: Go, Sir Andrew. Scout for him at the corner of the orchard. Draw and swear horrible. Away! *(Sir Andrew leaves at a trot.)* Now I will fright them both. *(All laugh.)*

Fabian: (Looking offstage) Here he comes with your niece. *(The three leave quickly before Viola and Olivia enter.)*

Olivia: (Sadly) I have said too much unto a heart of stone. And, I beseech you, come again tomorrow. *(Viola bows.)* Fare thee well. *(Olivia leaves, weeping.)*

Sir Toby: (To Viola as he enters with Fabian) Gentleman, God save thee. *(Pointing, with a heavy warning)* Thy interpreter attends thee at the orchard-end. Be quick and deadly.

Viola: (Horrified) I am sure no man hath any quarrel to me. What is he?

Sir Toby: He is knight, but he is a devil.

Viola: I am no fighter. I beseech you, to know of the knight what my offence to him is.

Sir Toby: I will do so. Signior Fabian, stay you by this gentleman till my return. *(He exits.)*

Viola: (To Fabian) Pray you sir, do you know of this matter?

Fabian: (Fiercely) He is, indeed, sir, most skillful, bloody and fatal. *(They stand to one side, watching fearfully.)*

Sir Toby: (Entering with Sir Andrew, he points to Viola.) Why, man, he's a very devil.

Sir Andrew: (Frightened) I'll not meddle with him. *(He stops on his side of the stage while Sir Toby goes to Viola to frighten her more.)*

Sir Toby: There's no remedy, sir. He will fight with you.

Viola: I do assure you, 'tis against my will.
(She draws her sword. It trembles.)

Viola: (Terrified) Pray God defend me!

Sir Toby: (Returning to Sir Andrew) Come, Sir Andrew, there's no remedy. Come on. *(Sir Andrew draws his sword timidly.)*

Viola: I do assure you, 'tis against my will. *(She draws her sword. It trembles.)*

(The two cowardly fighters circle. Viola taps her sword against Sir Andrew's, and he yelps. She covers her eyes with her hand. They circle again. At that moment, Antonio enters, mistaking Viola for Sebastian.)

Antonio: (To Viola) Put up your sword. *(To Sir Andrew)* If this young gentleman has done offence, I take the fault on me. *(He draws his sword. Sir Toby draws his also.)*

Fabian: Hold! Here come the officers. *(All put up their swords as the officers enter.)*

Announcer 2: The police come to arrest Antonio as an enemy of the country.

First Officer: Antonio, I arrest thee at the suit of Count Orsino. *(He takes him by the arm.)*

Antonio: (To Viola) I must obey. This comes with seeking you. My necessity makes me to ask you for some of that money.

Viola: (Puzzled) What money, sir? I'll lend you something. *(She takes out a few coins.)*

Antonio: (Grieved) Will you deny those kindnesses that I have done for you?

Viola: I know of none. Nor know I you by voice or any feature.

Second Officer: Come sir, I pray you, go.

Antonio: (Upset, pointing to Viola) This youth that you see here I snatched one half out of the jaws of death. *(To Viola)* O, Sebastian, shame. *(The officers drag him off.)*

Viola: (Excited) He named Sebastian. *(She touches her clothes.)* My brother went in this fashion, color, ornament. For him I imitate. O, if it prove, tempests are kind, and salt waves fresh in love! *(She leaves happily.)*

Sir Toby: (Frowning) A very dishonest boy, and a coward.

Sir Andrew: I'll after him and beat him. *(All follow Viola offstage.)*

ACT IV

(Servants remove the trees and put up the city wall. On comes the Clown, dragging Sebastian to see Olivia. Sebastian protests and struggles.)

Announcer 1: The twins cause more confusion.

Clown: Will you believe that I am sent for you?

Sebastian: Go to, go to. Let me be clear of thee.

Clown: (Sarcastically) No, I do not know you; nor I am not sent to you by my lady, to bid you come speak with her, nor your name is not Master Cesario, *(Tapping his nose)* nor this is not my nose neither. Nothing that is so, is so.

Sir Andrew: (Entering angrily and marching to Sebastian) Now, sir, there's for you! *(He strikes him.)*

Sebastian: (Hitting back) Why, there's for thee, and there, and there! Are all the people mad?

Sir Toby: (Entering with Fabian and drawing his sword) Come on sir; hold.

Olivia: (Entering, shocked) Hold, Toby! On thy life, I charge thee hold! Out of my sight! *(To Sebastian, tenderly)* Be not offended, dear Cesario. *(To Sir Toby)* Be gone. *(Sir Toby and the others leave reluctantly.)*

(She takes Sebastian's arm. He smiles with delight at this lovely stranger.) I prithee, gentle friend, go with me to my house.

Sebastian: I am mad, or else this is a dream. *(He lets her lead him off, grinning happily.)*

Announcer 2: Now the jokers begin to tease Malvolio, who has been put in a prison because he seemed crazy.

(Maria enters with the Clown. She carries a priest's black robe, a cross on a chain, and a beard.)

Maria: Nay, put on this gown and this beard; make him believe thou art Sir Topas the curate. I'll call Sir Toby. *(She waves to Sir Toby to enter while the Clown gets dressed. Sir Toby carries his beer mug.)*

Sir Toby: (To the Clown) Jove bless thee, Master Parson. *(He points to the alcove.)* To him, Sir Topas.

Clown: (Calling in an old man's voice) What ho, I say. Peace in this prison!

(On comes Malvolio, bringing on stage his prison bars and blinking as if he has been in the dark.)

Malvolio: Who calls there?

Clown: Sir Topas the curate, who comes to visit Malvolio the lunatic.

Malvolio: Good Sir Topas, do not think I am mad. They have laid me here in hideous darkness.

Clown: Madman, I say there is no darkness but ignorance. Fare thee well.

(Malvolio begins to cry loudly and beat at the bars. No one laughs. They look sorry for him.)

Announcer 1: The pranksters feel the joke has gone too far, and Olivia is too angry with them.

Sir Toby: (Uncomfortably) I would we were well rid of this knavery. If he may be delivered, I would he were. *(He waves his mug.)* I am now so far in offence with my niece that I cannot pursue with any safety this sport.

(He starts to drink and looks at Maria. She shakes her head. He shakes his head. Slowly he gives her the mug, which she puts down on a bench. Then, sober at last, he smiles and exits with his arm around a happy Maria.)

Clown: (Singing in his own voice as he takes off his disguise) "Hey, Robin, jolly Robin, Tell me how thy lady does."

Malvolio: (Calling) Fool.

Clown: Who calls, ha? *(He pretends to discover him.)* Master Malvolio?

Malvolio: Good fool, some ink, paper, and light; and convey what I will set down to my lady.

Clown: I will help you. But tell me true, are you not mad indeed?

Malvolio: Believe me, I am not.

Clown: (Kindly) I will fetch you light and paper and ink.

(The Clown leaves with the mug and his disguise, while Malvolio moves his gaol [jail] bars offstage.)

Sebastian: (Entering in a happy daze, looking at the sky and also at a ring.) This is the air. That is the glorious sun. This pearl she gave me. Yet 'tis not madness. Where's Antonio then? I could not find him at the Elephant. *(He shakes his head.)* I am mad, or else the lady's mad. *(Looking off-stage)* But here the lady comes. *(Olivia enters with a Priest.)*

Announcer 2: Olivia wants to marry Viola's twin.

Olivia: (Breathless with love) Blame not this haste of mine. If you mean well, now go with me and with this holy man. Plight me the full assurance of your faith. What do you say?

Sebastian: (With a smile of love) I'll follow this good man and go with you. And having sworn truth, ever will be true.

(The Priest joins their hands and makes the Sign of the Cross over them. Then he turns and leads them offstage to be married.)

ACT V

(From one side of the stage comes Viola with the Duke, and from the other come the officers with Antonio.)

Announcer 1: Matters get more confused.

Viola: (Pointing Antonio out to the Duke) Here comes the man, sir, that did rescue me.

Duke: That face of his I do remember well. *(To Antonio)* Notable pirate. What foolish boldness brought thee to thine enemies?

Antonio: (Angrily pointing at Viola) Orsino, noble sir, that most ingrateful boy there by your side, from the rude sea his life I gave him. His false cunning denied me mine own purse, which I had recommended to his use not half an hour before.

Viola: (Shaking her head) How can this be?

Duke: When came he to this town?

Antonio: Today, my lord.

Duke: (Seeing Olivia enter) Here comes the Countess; now Heaven walks on Earth. *(To Antonio, harshly)* But fellow, thy words are madness. Three months this youth hath tended upon me. *(Antonio is amazed.)*

Olivia: (To Viola) Cesario, you do not keep promise with me.

Duke: (To Olivia) Gracious Olivia, still so cruel?

Olivia: Still so constant, lord.

Duke: (In despair) What shall I do? *(To Viola)* Come, boy, with me. *(He and Viola start to leave.)*

Olivia: Whither, my lord? Cesario, husband, stay.

Duke: Husband? *(To Viola)* Her husband, sirrah?

Viola: No, my lord, not I.

Olivia (Shocked, but quickly relieved as the Priest enters.) O, welcome, Father! Father, what dost thou know hath newly passed between this youth and me?

Priest: (Happily) A contract of eternal bond of love, strengthened by interchangement of your rings, and all the ceremony sealed by my testimony. *(He beams at the "newlyweds.")*

Duke: (Furious at Viola) O thou dissembling cub. Farewell and take her. *(He starts to leave.)*

Viola: My lord, I do protest.

(At this moment Sir Andrew enters, followed by Sir Toby. Both are bloody from swordfights.)

Sir Andrew: For the love of God, a surgeon! Send one to Sir Toby.

Olivia: Who has done this, Sir Andrew?

Sir Andrew: The Count's gentleman, one Cesario. He's the very devil.

Duke: My gentleman Cesario?

Sir Andrew: (Seeing Viola) Here he is! You broke my head for nothing.

Viola: I never hurt you. You drew your sword upon me without cause.

Sir Toby: 'Has hurt me and there's the end on it.

Olivia: Get him to bed, and let his hurt be looked to. *(She glares at Viola, who shakes her head.)*

Sebastian: (Entering and going directly to Olivia, without noticing Viola.) I am sorry, madam, I have hurt your kinsman. *(He stops and looks puzzled at her amazement.)* You throw a strange regard upon me, and by that I do perceive it hath offended you. *(Romantically)* Pardon me, sweet one, even for the vows we made each other but so late ago.

Duke: (Looking from Sebastian to Viola and back.) One face, one voice, one habit, and two persons.

Sebastian: (Seeing Antonio) Antonio! How have the hours tortured me since I have lost thee!

Antonio: (Uncertainly) Sebastian, how have you made division of yourself? *(He points to Viola. Sebastian goes to her, and they look each other up and down with growing delight.)*

Sebastian: I had a sister whom the blind waves have devoured. What kin are you to me?

Viola: Sebastian was my father. Such a Sebastian was my brother too, so went he to his watery tomb.

Sebastian: Were you a woman, I should my tears let fall upon your cheek, and say, "Thrice welcome, drowned Viola!"

Viola: I am Viola. *(They hug each other happily.)*

Sebastian: (To Olivia) So comes it, lady, you are betrothed both to a maid and man. *(He smiles.)*

Duke: (To Viola) Boy, thou hast said to me a thousand times thou never shouldst love woman like to me. *(Viola blushes.)* Give me thy hand. *(She shyly puts her hand in his, and he smiles.)* And let me see thee in thy woman's weeds. *(She smiles broadly then.)*

Announcer 2: But the Captain who kept Viola's dress has been put in prison by Malvolio.

Viola: The Captain that did bring me first on shore hath my maid's garments. He is now in durance, at Malvolio's suit.

Olivia: Fetch Malvolio hither. *(She stops as she sees the Clown and Fabian enter.)* And yet, alas, they say, he's much distract. *(She taps her head and calls to the Clown.)* How does he, sirrah?

Clown: (Showing her a note) Truly, madam, he has here writ a letter to you. *(He opens and reads it.)* "By the Lord, madam, you wrong me. I have your own letter that induced me to the semblance I put on. The madly used Malvolio."

Olivia: Did he write this? *(The Clown nods.)* Fabian, bring him hither. (Fabian leaves.)

Announcer 1: The Duke proposes to Viola.

Duke: (To Viola) Since you called me master for so long, here is my hand. You shall from this time be your master's mistress. *(They clasp hands happily.)*

(Fabian enters with Malvolio, who is in a rage.)

Malvolio: (To Olivia, waving a letter.) Madam, you have done me wrong. Notorious wrong. *(Thrusting the letter at her)* Lady, peruse that letter. You must not deny it is your hand. Tell me why you bade me come smiling and cross-gartered to you, to put on yellow stockings. And, acting this, why have you suffered me to be imprisoned. Tell me why.

Olivia: (Scanning the letter) Alas, Malvolio, this is not my writing. 'Tis Maria's hand.

Fabian: Good madam, hear me speak. Most freely I confess, myself and Toby set this device against Malvolio here. Maria writ the letter at Sir Toby's great importance, in recompense whereof—he hath married her.

(Malvolio, hearing the news, huffs and puffs, stiffly biting his lips. The others watch, trying not to laugh at the Twelfth Night joke.

Malvolio: (Weakly) I'll be revenged on the whole pack of you! *(He exits, sniffing proudly.)*

Olivia: (Sympathetically) He hath been most notoriously abused.

Duke: (In a kind voice to Fabian) Pursue him, and entreat him to a peace. *(As Fabian leaves, the Duke takes Viola's arm.)* A solemn combination shall be made of our dear souls. Cesario, come. For so you shall be, while you are a man. But when in other habits you are seen, Orsino's mistress and his fancy's queen. *(All cheer loudly.)*

Announcer 2: The Clown's song says a foolish little boy only plays, but no one wants a foolish man. People have enough troubles, like the wind and the rain.

(As the Clown sings, the characters parade around the stage, joined by a happy Sir Toby and Maria, Fabian with a pacified Malvolio, and others, coming forward to take curtain calls. All can join in the singing if they wish.)

Clown: (Sings)

When that I was and a little tiny boy,
  With hey, ho, the wind and the rain,
A foolish thing was but a toy,
  For the rain it raineth every day.

But when I came to man's estate,
  With hey, ho, the wind and the rain,
'Gainst knaves and thieves men shut their gate,
  For the rain it raineth every day.

But when I came, alas, to wive,
  With hey, ho, the wind and the rain,
By swaggering could I never thrive
For the rain it raineth every day.

A great while ago the world begun,
  With hey, ho, the wind and the rain,
But that's all one, our play is done,
  And we'll strive to please you every day.

*(He bows and waves his cap, as all leave,
singing together.)*

When That I Was and a Little Tiny Boy

Traditional

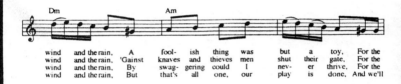

When that I was and a lit- tle ti- ny boy With-- hey, ho, the
But when I came to man's es- tate, With-- hey, ho, the
But when I came, a- las! to wive, With-- hey, ho, the
(A) great while a-go the world be- gun, With-- hey, ho, the

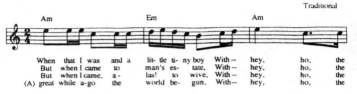

wind and the rain, A fool- ish thing was but a toy, For the
wind and the rain, 'Gainst knaves and thieves men shut their gate, For the
wind and the rain, By swag- gering could I nev- er thrive, For the
wind and the rain, But that's all one, our play is done, And we'll

CHORUS:

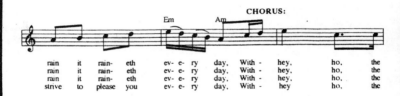

rain it rain- eth ev- e- ry day, With - hey, ho, the
rain it rain- eth ev- e- ry day, With - hey, ho, the
rain it rain- eth ev- e- ry day, With - hey, ho, the
strive to please you ev- e- ry day, With - hey ho, the

wind - and the rain, For the rain it rain- eth ev- e- ry day.
wind - and the rain, For the rain it rain- eth ev- e- ry day.
wind - and the rain, For the rain it rain- eth ev- e- ry day.
wind - and the rain, For the rain it rain- eth ev- e- ry day.